# WHO WORDS

shoppers

seller

by Carrie B. Sheely

PEBBLE
a capstone imprint

# Who is it?

Is it your friends? Maybe it's the mail carrier. Who else could it be? Let words tell you who it is!

mail carrier

friends

pals

dad

daddy

papa

father

sister

mother

mom

mama

mommy

brother

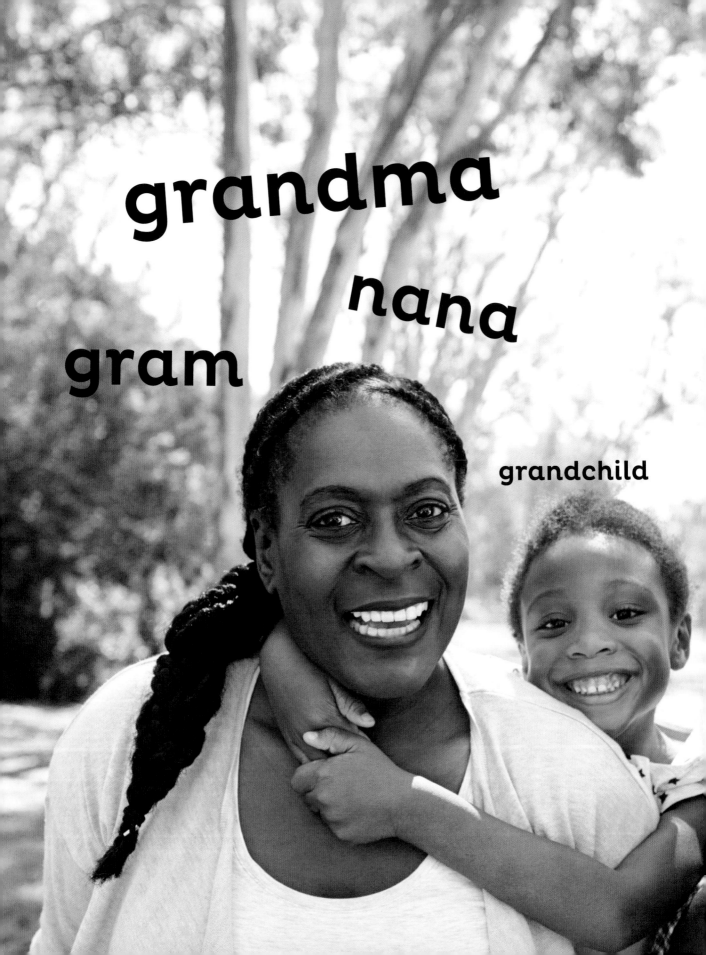

grandma

nana

gram

grandchild

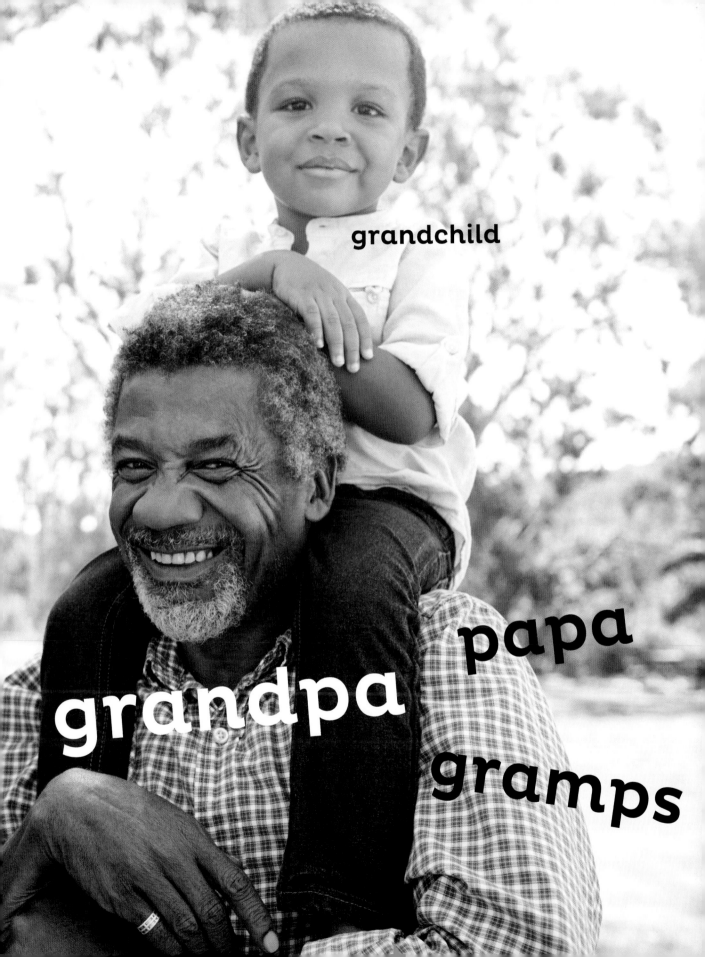

grandchild

grandpa

papa

gramps

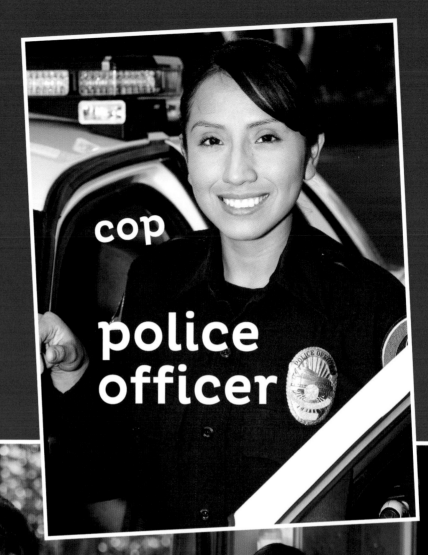

cop

police
officer

EMTs

paramedics

firefighter

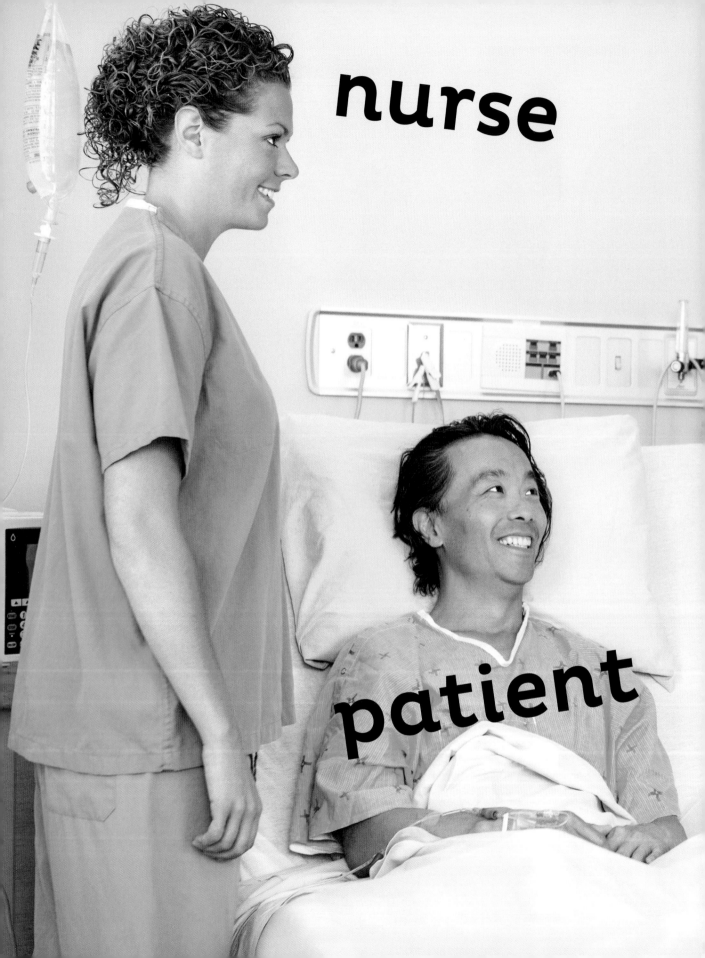

nurse

patient

doctors

teacher

Mr. Martin

student

students

kids

librarian

SCHOOL BUS

bus
driver

astronaut

Space walker

# dancers

# ballerinas

construction workers

house builders

masons

# road roller driver

lifeguard

swimmers

diver

marine biologist

scientist

vets

veterinarians

animal
trainer

zookeeper

teammates

Emily

Jada

soccer players

Susie

coach

Simone Biles

gymnast

**crowd**

Who else do
you see?

stunt rider

# skydiver

# climber

# football players

## referee

quarterback

Drew Brees

Who else do you see?

Pebble Sprout is published by Pebble,
an imprint of Capstone.
1710 Roe Crest Drive
North Mankato, Minnesota 56003
www.capstonepub.com

**Library of Congress Cataloging-in-Publication Data is
available on the Library of Congress website.**
ISBN: 978-1-9771-1309-2 (library binding)
ISBN: 978-1-9771-1825-7 (paperback)
ISBN: 978-1-9771-1315-3 (eBook PDF)

Summary: Through engaging photos,
introduces nouns that name people.

**Image Credits**
Dreamstime: Michael Bush, 17; iStockphoto: FatCamera, 20,
fstop123, 18 (top), simonkr, 1; NASA: 14–15; Newscom: Icon
Sportswire/Jeffrey Vest, 30–31; Shutterstock: AnnaElizabeth
Photography, 22 (bottom), Gerain0812, 28, Greg Epperson,
29 (bottom), hedgehog94, 22 (top), JGA, cover, John Roman
Images, 8 (top), Kseniia Vorobeva, 16, Leonard Zhukovsky,
26–27, LightField Studios, 13 (bottom), Mauricio Graiki,
29 (top), meunierd, 23, michaeljung, 8 (bottom), Monkey
Business Images, 4–5, 6–7, 12, 24–25, Nicole Helgason, 21,
Rawpixel, 13 (top), Robert Kneschke, 3, sattahipbeach, 2,
Sergei Butorin, 18 (bottom), Tyler Olson, 9, 10–11, Vadim
Ratnikov, 19

**Editorial Credits**
Designer: Juliette Peters
Media Researcher: Svetlana Zhurkin
Production Specialist: Katy LaVigne

Printed and bound in the USA.
PA99

# Titles in this set:

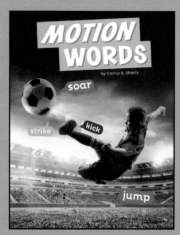

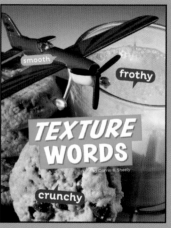

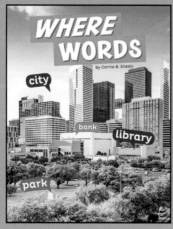